Bamboo Ballet

SH-WOO-OO-OOSH. It sounded like the wind was whispering.

Ping swirled his arms in time with the beautiful sound.

SH-WI-SH. The bamboo rustled.

Ping's body swayed with the lovely sound.

He was so busy swirling and swaying that he almost fell out of the tree!

The next day, Ping could hardly wait to climb to the top of the bamboo. But he had not even started to climb when he froze.

PLIP, PLIP, PLOP!

'What wonderful new sound is this?' he thought.

It was raindrops plip, plip, plopping in the forest.

Ping wriggled his bottom. He swayed and swirled with the lovely sounds.

Moving to the sounds of the forest felt wonderful!

"Ping, what are you doing?" the other little

pandas asked.

"Ping is dancing," Elder Panda grumbled.

"Pandas need to be still and eat bamboo."

But Ping couldn't be still!

He stood on the tips of his paws and leapt into the air. He swayed and swirled and waved his arms. He shook his bottom and kicked his feet.

Elder Panda shook her head. "Dancing is not what pandas do," she said.

Each day, Ping's friends peeped through the bamboo and watched Ping dancing.

They thought dancing looked so much fun!

"Ping, please will you teach us to dance?" they asked. "We want to dance the bamboo ballet too!"

"Of course!" said Ping.

All the little pandas learned to listen to the sounds of the bamboo forest.

Ping taught them the moves of bamboo ballet.

They stood on the tips of their paws and leapt into the air. They swayed and swirled, waving their arms. They shook their bottoms and kicked their feet.

The little pandas had so much fun, but they made so much noise!

Elder Panda heard them! She went to

investigate.

She crept towards a clearing in the forest

and peeped through the bamboo.

None of the little pandas noticed Elder Panda

watching them dance.

As Elder Panda watched, her paws tapped.

She felt the beat of the bamboo ballet!

"A panda *must* eat bamboo all day long!"

Elder Panda muttered to herself. "Dancing is

not what pandas do. What if the humans see?"

More and more pandas joined in with the bamboo ballet.

Ping taught his mum to sway and swirl.

He showed his Great Uncle Feng how to shake his bottom.

Even Grandma Ying wiggled a paw.

Elder Panda peeped through the bamboo and watched. Oh, how she felt the beat of the bamboo ballet!

"But dancing is *not* what pandas do," she grumbled to herself. "What if somebody sees?"

Soon, Ping and all the other pandas were so busy dancing the bamboo ballet that Elder Panda was left all alone eating bamboo.

SH-WOO-OO-OOSH.
SH-WI-SH.
PLIP-PLIP-PLOP!
She heard the sounds of the forest.

Her paws tapped and her claws clicked.

She couldn't resist the beat of the

bamboo ballet. Elder Panda danced!

"What's that tapping and clicking sound?" Ping asked.

All the pandas stopped dancing. They crept through the forest and peeped through the bamboo.

"Elder Panda is doing the bamboo ballet!" cried Ping.

Now, *all* the pandas in the forest danced the bamboo ballet together. It was so much fun.

But they made so much noise!

Some passing explorers heard them.

The explorers crept into the forest.

But when they reached the clearing,

all the pandas were doing

what pandas do...

Quiz

1. What did Elder Panda think pandas should do all day?
a) Eat bamboo
b) Sleep
c) Climb trees

2. What was the first sound Ping heard?
a) The rain
b) Birds singing
c) The wind

3. What sound did the rain make?
a) PLIP, PLIP, PLOP!
b) DRIP, DRIP, DROP!
c) SLIP, SLIP, SLOP!

4. How did Great Uncle Feng dance?

a) He wiggled his paw

b) He shook his bottom

c) He swayed his arms

5. What did the explorers see the pandas doing?

a) Dancing

b) Singing

c) Eating bamboo

Turn over for answers

Book Bands for Guided Reading

The Institute of Education book banding system is a scale of colours that reflects the various levels of reading difficulty. The bands are assigned by taking into account the content, the language style, the layout and phonics. Word, phrase and sentence level work is also taken into consideration.

Maverick Early Readers are a bright, attractive range of books covering the pink to white bands. All of these books have been book banded for guided reading to the industry standard and edited by a leading educational consultant.

Pink
Red
Yellow
Blue
Green
Orange
Turquoise
Purple
Gold
White

To view the whole Maverick Readers scheme, visit our website at www.maverickearlyreaders.com

Or scan the QR code above to view our scheme instantly!

Quiz Answers: 1a, 2c, 3a, 4b, 5c